ANIMAL SAFARI

Iguanas

by Chris Bowman

BLASTOFF! READERS

BELLWETHER MEDIA • MINNEAPOLIS, MN

Note to Librarians, Teachers, and Parents:

Blastoff! Readers are carefully developed by literacy experts and combine standards-based content with developmentally appropriate text.

Level 1 provides the most support through repetition of high-frequency words, light text, predictable sentence patterns, and strong visual support.

Level 2 offers early readers a bit more challenge through varied simple sentences, increased text load, and less repetition of high-frequency words.

Level 3 advances early-fluent readers toward fluency through increased text and concept load, less reliance on visuals, longer sentences, and more literary language.

Level 4 builds reading stamina by providing more text per page, increased use of punctuation, greater variation in sentence patterns, and increasingly challenging vocabulary.

Level 5 encourages children to move from "learning to read" to "reading to learn" by providing even more text, varied writing styles, and less familiar topics.

Whichever book is right for your reader, Blastoff! Readers are the perfect books to build confidence and encourage a love of reading that will last a lifetime!

This edition first published in 2015 by Bellwether Media, Inc.

No part of this publication may be reproduced in whole or in part without written permission of the publisher. For information regarding permission, write to Bellwether Media, Inc., Attention: Permissions Department, 5357 Penn Avenue South, Minneapolis, MN 55419.

Library of Congress Cataloging-in-Publication Data

Bowman, Chris, 1990- author.
  Iguanas / by Chris Bowman.
    pages cm. – (Blastoff! Readers. Animal Safari)
  Includes bibliographical references and index.
  Summary: "Developed by literacy experts for students in kindergarten through grade three, this book introduces iguanas to young readers through leveled text and related photos"– Provided by publisher.
  Audience: Ages 5-8.
  Audience: K to grade 3.
  ISBN 978-1-62617-164-0 (hardcover : alk. paper)
  1. Iguanas–Juvenile literature. I. Title. II. Series: Blastoff! Readers. 1, Animal Safari.
  QL666.L25B69 2015
  597.95'42–dc23
                                                            2014034749

Printed in the United States of America, North Mankato, MN.

Contents

What Are Iguanas?

Iguanas are **reptiles** with long tails. They have hard **spines** on their backs.

Loose skin hangs below their necks. Iguanas can puff out this skin.

Where Iguanas Live

Most iguanas live in **rain forests**. Others are found on beaches or in **deserts**.

Iguanas spend most of their time on branches. Their sharp **claws** help them climb.

claw

In the Trees

Iguanas eat leaves, fruits, and flowers from the branches.

They stay on the
branches to hide
from **predators**.
Snakes and large
birds hunt them.

Sometimes predators get too close. Iguanas hit them with their tails. They also jump into water.

Males, Females, and Babies

Male iguanas fight over females. They bob their heads. Then they **wrestle**.

Females lay eggs in **burrows**. Then they leave the nests. **Hatchlings** are on their own!

Glossary

burrows—holes or tunnels in the ground that some animals dig

claws—sharp, curved nails at the ends of an animal's toes

deserts—dry lands with little rain

hatchlings—baby iguanas

predators—animals that hunt other animals for food

rain forests—warm forests that receive a lot of rain

reptiles—cold-blooded animals that have backbones and scales

spines—sharp points on the bodies of some animals

wrestle—to fight by holding and pushing

To Learn More

AT THE LIBRARY

Hansen, Grace. *Iguanas*. Minneapolis, Minn.: ABDO Kids, 2014.

Schuetz, Kari. *Chameleons*. Minneapolis, Minn.: Bellwether Media, Inc., 2014.

Schuh, Mari. *Iguanas*. Minneapolis, Minn.: Jump!, 2015.

ON THE WEB

Learning more about iguanas is as easy as 1, 2, 3.

1. Go to www.factsurfer.com.

2. Enter "iguanas" into the search box.

3. Click the "Surf" button and you will see a list of related web sites.

With factsurfer.com, finding more information is just a click away.

Index

The images in this book are reproduced through the courtesy of: fivespots, front cover; Rattanachat Suppol, p. 5; Turau, p. 7; apiguide, p. 9 (top); MJ Prototype, p. 9 (bottom left); sunsinger, p. 9 (bottom center); Jane Rix, p. 9 (bottom right); Sabena Jane Blackbird/ Alamy, p. 11 (top); WitthayaP, p. 11 (bottom); Ingo Schulz/ Glow Images, p. 13 (top); Evgeniya Uvarova, p. 13 (bottom left); Donatella Tandelli, p. 13 (bottom center); Kurkul, p. 13 (bottom right); Malcolm Schuyl/ Alamy, p. 15 (top); nattanan726, p. 15 (bottom left); MarcusVDT, p. 15 (bottom right); Tony Crocetta/ Biosphoto, p. 17; David Thyberg, p. 19; bluedogroom, p. 21.